Letters to a First-Time Novelist

Angela Lam

Copyright © 2025 by Angela Lam
All rights reserved.

Publisher: Gross Productions
Cover Art: Unseen Studio
Cover Designer: Angela Lam
Proofreader: Judy Zweifel, Judy's Proofreading

No part of this book may be used or reproduced in any manner whatsoever without written permission from the publisher, except in the case of brief quotations embodied in critical articles or reviews.

Print ISBN: 979-8-9857935-9-8

For My Students

Thank you for the honor of trusting me with your heart, your soul, and your stories.

Also by Angela Lam

NOVELS

Legs

Out of Balance

Blood Moon Rising

The Divorce Planner

Friends First

The Women of the Crush Series

Last Chance

NOVELLA

No Amends

SHORT STORIES

The Human Act and Other Stories

Water Baby and Other Stories

MEMOIRS

Red Eggs and Good Luck

The Fool and the Magician

Think of your story as a sculpture.

The first draft is getting the clay on the table.

Introduction

With the advent of email, we have lost the art of letter writing. Gone are the days when you could luxuriate at the desk with a pen in hand, mulling over the words you want to communicate to a beloved. Nowadays, a quick email response is sent without further thought.

Through my studies with the Buddhist nun Pema Chodron, I have learned a technique that has transformed my life—pause practice. Like most Buddhist practices, the concept is simple, but without training, the application is hard to do in the moment. Here it is—whenever I am bombarded by mental chatter, devastating news, or an overwhelming emotion, I stop and take three conscious breaths. That's it. Just breathe. In and out, in and out, in and out. Before I even complete the third breath, I step into the gap between what I was feeling and what I am feeling right now. This fresh look at novel writing is what I wished to capture, and I could only do it through letter writing.

Because we are uncomfortable with spaciousness, we often fill it with whatever is habitual to us, from self-deprecating thoughts to hopeful fantasies. Very rarely do we follow our original thoughts, the ones we embraced as children playing in the sandbox. But when we write the first draft of anything, especially a novel, we need to embody that carefree place where everything is possible.

I kept this truth in mind when I sat down to write the first draft of these letters in a lined journal with my favorite purple gel pen. I resisted the temptation to cross out, rewrite, or question. Each day I composed a new letter to the same imaginary student, my ideal reader. I drew from my experiences with former students, recalling the most asked questions and answering them as truthfully as I could from my own experience or my knowledge from experts. Some of the letters are craft-based. Some are motivational. Others are a combination of practical and inspirational advice. All of them cover the journey of writing an initial draft of a novel, from concept to denouncement. I did my best to cover everything.

While this book does not replace one of my live classes where students receive accountability and community, it does offer you the same techniques and encouragement to get you through the first draft.

Happy writing,

Angela

P.S. At the end of each letter is a postscript with exercises you may try or questions you may wish to journal.

Ready, Set...

Dear Future Author,

Yes, "future" because you have not begun to write. You are contemplating writing.

Maybe you have a bucket list or a New Year's resolution: write a novel.

Maybe you have written short stories and want to expand into a longer form. Maybe you're a screenwriter and want to try a different vehicle to share your stories, one in which you are writer, producer, director, and actor. Maybe you've seized upon an idea, or an idea has taken hold of you and won't let go. You must write this story.

And, so, we begin.

First, you must create a writing habit. Call it a schedule. For those of you who are working, you may refer to writing as your part-time job. For those of you who are retired, you may prefer to call it your play hours. Whatever you call it, commit to showing up to write at the designated time. Consistency is the first step. Without it, you will flounder on finishing your first draft.

You may have to try out a few days/nights and times before you discover the right fit for your current lifestyle. Yes, this schedule is subject to change as your life and your writing evolve. Be flexible. Be open. When I wrote my first novel, I was nineteen years old, attending school full-time and working part-time and living at my parents' home. I wrote at my boyfriend's house on his Commodore computer. When I wrote my first novel under contract, I was twenty-eight years old, pregnant with my second child, and working full-time with a husband and a disabled son. I woke up an hour earlier than everyone in the household to write five days a week. Sometimes I wrote more on the weekends and other times I didn't write at all. Find what works.

Please, do not think too far ahead. You only need to know when you will be writing this week. At the end of this week, you will set your schedule for the following week, and so on. This process allows you to accommodate the natural ebb and flow of life, accounting for variances in work schedule, family obligations, social events, and the occasional unexpected moments no one can predict.

Finally, be kind to yourself. Writing a novel is a new adventure, a commitment, an exploration that combines who you are and what you wish to accomplish. During this journey, you will discover who you are as a writer, what your writing process entails, and the heart of the story only you can write.

Do not be concerned with readers at this point. Why not? Readers are the final step. Their opinion as well as the opinions of the publishing community only muddy the waters of your creative well. You need the freedom to write "a shitty first draft" as Anne Lamott espouses in *Bird by Bird*. Students often ask why I don't talk about writing to the market when I discuss the first draft. Why should I? No one except you will see this initial manuscript. It would be like showing an audience a slab of clay or a primed canvas. People will superimpose their opinions, give advice, and try to shape the proposed project. What you need is to hunker down and work as quickly as possible to capture the initial spark on the page. Once the draft is done, take a moment to celebrate your success. Put the manuscript aside for as long as possible. I suggest four to six weeks. Continue with your writing practice. Or if you're depleted, channel your interests elsewhere. I often catch up on reading recently published books or knock out a few acrylic paintings. Sometimes I do nothing but sleep. Once your creative resources are replenished, examine your manuscript as a reader. Mark the places that took you out of the story. Add notes in the margin about any ideas you have on how to fix these bumps in the road. Write another draft keeping these thoughts in mind. Once you're satisfied you have done everything in your power to make this story sing, give it a final polish, correcting spelling, grammar, and punctuation. Then, and only then, seek counsel from a handful of trusted readers: maybe a teacher, a writing friend, or a beta reader in your genre.

But right now, resist the temptation to involve anyone in this process. I don't care if your spouse, your best friend, or your siblings want to see your initial pages. Do not show them. Keep your head down and write.

Don't worry. I'll be with you throughout this process. I will do my best to anticipate any challenges you may encounter and answer any questions you may have. But at the end of the day, you must keep up your end of the bargain, and that is to write!

All the best,

Angela

P.S. Do you have a writing practice? What is it?

If you don't, take time over the next few weeks to develop one.

Here are some techniques to try:

1. Get up early and write for one hour. It's okay to make your favorite drink and put on some soothing music (or create a soundtrack for your novel). Just make sure to set a timer and keep writing until the time is up.
2. Stay up late and write. Some people are night owls and get more work done after everyone is asleep.
3. Write during your lunch break. If you have an hour, eat for the first half and write for the second half.
4. Create a do-it-yourself writing retreat on your day off. Block out four to eight hours and alternate between writing, walking, and reflecting.
5. Practice self-care. If you're tired, hungry, emotionally spent or wound up, you can't focus on writing well. Do what you need to do to get your body and mind in a good place to create. Eat a healthy meal, take a bath, nap for an hour, or visit a friend.
6. Get rid of the myth of the alcoholic writer. Hemingway, Kerouac, and others glamorized this type of writing practice. Alcohol is poison. If you need help relaxing, try exercise or meditation. If you need help trusting the creative process, spend time with a child. Toddlers tap directly into that crazy river of creation we all seek. And they do it by just being themselves.

...Write.

Dear Author,

Yes, author, because you are writing a book.

What is the official definition of author? *Webster's New World Dictionary* defines it as "one who makes or creates something; a writer of books."

But books don't count as "books" unless they are published, right?

Webster's New World Dictionary defines book as "a printed work on sheets of paper bound together, usually between protective covers." Granted, this edition of the dictionary was published before eBooks and audiobooks entered the market.

Regardless of the definition of author and book, I assume you want to publish this novel you are writing. Therefore, I will operate out of the law of attraction or the sales technique of assuming the close or the optimistic enthusiasm that this book you are writing will one day find a home with a publisher (or self-publisher) and into the public (or readers).

Why am I so optimistic when eighty-one percent of Americans want to write a book but less than one percent of Americans sell the book they've written according to recent surveys? Because you are here, reading this letter. You have committed to this story. Through devotion and hard work, the story will manifest one word at a time.

Even if you and your book fall into the ninety-nine percent of books written and never published, there is still value in having written a novel.

First, you will discover something about yourself. When you face the blank page on a regular basis, you eventually write through the detritus to uncover the gems lying at the bottom of your soul. These nuggets of wisdom emerge through your characters and storylines.

Second, storytelling is inherent in each of us. From primitive cave drawings to oral histories, people tell stories to connect and share knowledge from one generation to the next. For me, as well as many others, writing is as essential as breathing.

Third, writing is a form of entertainment. We all need a reprieve from daily living. Why not escape into a story?

Fourth, writing a novel is a commitment. A short story may take only a day to write. A novel may take weeks, months, or years to complete. Going the distance requires loyalty, tenacity, passion, discipline, and focus, especially in the face of any challenges life may throw at you along the way. I tell my students it's the leap from dating to a long-term relationship.

Finally, writing is fun. I compare it with playing in a sandbox. You're free to create whatever you want to create. You can experiment with sounds and syllables. Make up new words. Try different formats. Blend genres. Mix fact with fiction. Tell a story backwards, from the ending to the beginning. Toss around the timeframe, so the story comes together like a 1,000-piece puzzle. The choice is yours.

Sure, you'll run into resistance, both external and internal. My brother-in-law, a standup comedian and fellow author, suggested I read *The War of Art: Break Through the*

Blocks and Win Your Inner Creative Battles by Steven Pressfield when I mentioned I was between projects. Now this little manual is my go-to reference for students who have stopped and started but never finished writing a novel.

It's time to take away your excuses. Don't have enough time? Cut down on binge-watching TV. Not enough ideas? Take a moment in your life you wish would have ended differently and rewrite the experience from another person's point of view. Not enough skill? Find an author who has mastered the skill you wish to learn and dissect their storytelling, scene by scene. Too afraid to fail? We learn more from what does not work than we do from what does. Still scared? Go for it anyway.

You're not alone. I am with you. I've walked this path several times. I'll show you the way…one word at a time.

I believe in you.

Now it is time to believe in yourself.

You are an author.

You will finish this novel (and perhaps many more) and find a publisher (if you want).

Till next time,

Angela

P.S. Do you believe in yourself and your writing goals? In my opinion, it is easier to achieve your goals if you believe it is possible.

Here are some steps to eliminate your excuses and focus on your novel:

1. When people ask what you do, tell them you're a writer. See how they react. More importantly, watch your reaction. How does it feel? Do you embrace the label like a warm and well-loved sweater, or do you reject it like someone else's coat? Keep calling yourself a writer until the phrase becomes comfortable.
2. Break down your writing goals into daily or weekly bite-sized tasks. Now block out that time in your calendar. Make your writing habit as important as your doctor's appointment or your visit to relatives or your book club meeting or your volunteer work or cleaning your house or caring for your family or your nine-to-five job. If you don't carve out the time, you won't get the writing done.
3. Treat yourself each time you accomplish your daily or weekly writing goals. The treat can be something small—a cup of coffee, a new nail polish, or lunch with a friend. The important thing is to celebrate your successes.
4. If you don't meet your goals, then examine why you failed and then make necessary adjustments. Sometimes we fail because of things outside of our control: the car breaks, the children get sick, the quarterly reports require overtime. Other times we fail because of our own shortcomings: we squander our time on social media, TV, or other mindless tasks or we cancel our commitment to write to make time for someone or something else. If the failure is caused by an outside circumstance, acknowledge it and let it go. Don't beat yourself up. If the failure is caused by your choices, then examine your motives. Is writing your novel a priority? Do you feel guilty taking time away from your other responsibilities to pursue your dreams? Once you discover the root of

your concern, you can address and solve the issue. If writing is important, then commit the time to show yourself it's important. If you feel guilty, then make sure your other responsibilities are taken care of before you devote time to your novel writing. We all have twenty-four hours each day. How you choose to spend those hours is your decision. Choose wisely and with compassion. You deserve to achieve your dreams. Start saying yes to yourself and your ambitions.

5. Find an accountability partner. It may be another writer or a family member or a friend who you can meet with regularly and share your goals and progress. Knowing you have to tell someone you've written makes it more likely you will write.

Ideas

Dear Writer,

You noticed I've changed my greeting to you again. Why?

You said you don't like the term "author" because you associate it with having published a novel. That's fine. I don't like pressure either. Going forward, I will address you as "writer" because writers write, and you are writing.

I know you say you're struggling to discover the right pace to complete 50,000 to 100,000 words, the typical range of a novel. If you use word count as your guide and you have a goal of finishing the first draft in a certain number of weeks, then you can divide the number of words by the number of weeks to determine your weekly pace. For example, if you aim for a 50,000-word novel and want to finish the first draft in 10 weeks, you need to average 5,000 words a week. Not every writer works that way, and not every book is written in ten weeks. For example, I measure my progress from scene to scene. If I write a scene a day, I am satisfied. My first novel took one year to draft. I didn't know what I was doing. It's a learning process. Now I can draft a novel in eight weeks. That transformation from one year to eight weeks took thirty years to master. Be kind to yourself. Write at your own pace. Some weeks you'll write more than others. The key is to find out what works for you and stick with it.

Now, let's discuss your subject matter. You don't need to know the entire story you want to write. You do need to have an idea from which to start. Need more help? I suggest examining what sparks your imagination: a person, a place, an experience, a conversation, or maybe even an obsession. When I stepped into Martine Inn, a bed-and-breakfast in Pacific Grove, California, I fell in love with the setting and envisioned a Hallmark-like novel taking place there. That experience was enough to fuel the first draft of a 53,000-word sweet contemporary romance, *Last Chance*, about a third-generation proprietor struggling to save his family's legacy and the childhood crush that inspires him. Another romance novel I drafted, *The Divorce Planner*, originated from my frustration over navigating the dissolution of my marriage. "Why don't they have divorce planners like they have wedding planners?" I complained. Who would want that occupation? The concept stuck, and I wrote 80,000 words about a woman working as a divorce planner whose daughter asks her to coordinate her wedding. My three-book series, *Women of the Crush*, was inspired by a friend who suggested I create a fictional world to encompass the experiences of my husband's senior softball tournament league. My paranormal romance, *Blood Moon Rising*, sprouted from the seeds of a short story about a suicidal vampire mother. Inspiration is everywhere. You need to discover what is yours.

Whatever you decide, make sure the concept holds enough energy to keep you motivated to continue writing to the end. Sometimes letting the idea simmer in the back of your mind for a few days or weeks is enough to test your commitment. Other times you might discover the right topic through trial and error. I've written books that have fizzled halfway through the first draft. Others didn't make it past the first chapter. The ideas that held the most passion, almost to the point of obsession, evolved into the stories that endured.

Why must you feel so captivated by your idea before you start?

The typical novel takes a certain amount of time to write. Afterward, that story will be revised. Once you sell the story, the editor will most likely request another revision. Finally, the story will undergo proofreading and last-minute corrections before being shipped to the printers. The entire process can take anywhere from one to several years. *The Divorce Planner*, from concept to publication, took three years of writing and revision. By the time the book hit the market, I never wanted to see it again. The novelty had worn off. If I didn't feel strongly about the story, I would have abandoned it once my future publisher asked for a revision *before* purchasing the story, which is a common publishing practice referred to as "revise and resubmit." Honestly, I don't remember how many drafts it took to complete that novel. I only know how depleted I felt afterward.

The seeds of your first novel might be different. But whatever it is, honor it, cherish it, and commit to exploring it. Be open to the limitless potential of this new beginning.

But beware of sharing your joy too soon. New writers often want to tell everyone they are working on a novel. They will share their ideas, including their outline and initial chapters. Family and friends will respond with feedback and suggestions. Sometimes this process is helpful. Most of the time it is not.

One of my students shared the first 2,000 words of her novel with family and friends who told her the idea was hackneyed and the writing was boring. She was crushed.

My poor student delivered her suffering to me. "This is the first piece of writing I want to turn into a novel and see published. I want someone to tell me the truth. Is my writing good enough? Is this story good enough? Am I good enough?"

I stared at her anguished expression, and my heart contracted with that familiar pain of craving validation. But she was paying me to coach her through the writing process, and I needed to be honest. "I can't make those judgments."

She widened her eyes.

"I need to see the whole story before I determine what works and what doesn't work."

She sniffled. "You mean you won't read anything I give you?"

"That's not what I'm saying." I inhaled deeply, considering how to phrase what I wanted to say. "I will not read your first draft because I believe what Anne Lamott says—we all write shitty first drafts. Let your first draft be shitty."

She snickered.

"Let everything hang out. Forget proper grammar. Just write the story down. You can fix everything later."

A smile flickered over her face.

"I want to see your notes on character, plot, and setting. I believe if you have those elements developed sufficiently, the rest of the writing will unfold naturally through cause and effect."

Her shoulders softened.

"I'll guide you through the first draft. I'll even give you tips to get through the second draft. After you polish the third draft, you can show it to everyone and ask for feedback."

She gulped. "Three drafts?"

I nodded. "It's not as hard as it sounds. The first draft is you discovering the story. The second draft is you shaping the elements into a well-written story. The third draft is you correcting the language, grammar, spelling, and punctuation."

By sheltering your partially written story from the eyes of readers, you increase the likelihood of finishing your manuscript.

My promise to you is to stick with you through the first draft.

Your promise to me is you will not quit.

Life will throw challenges along the way. Your car might break down. Your child might get sick. Your cat will rip up your favorite sweater. Your beloved might develop an annoying habit that will keep you up at night plotting revenge. But whatever catastrophe happens, adjust your goal and lower your expectations. Enjoy the process of writing. Delight in discovering the story only you can tell.

All the best,

Angela

P.S. I read somewhere that the number one reason people abandon writing a novel is because they mistook an idea for a story. An idea is a theme or a situation, such as love conquers all or homelessness. A story involves an individual facing a crisis that must be overcome, such as a husband finding a doctor who can diagnose and cure his wife's mysterious illness or an unhoused man who is an animal lover struggling with the decision of whether to kill a stray dog for sustenance. With this explanation in mind, test your subject matter. Do you have a person dealing with a specific problem that must be solved? If you discover your concept is too broad, such as finding a solution to climate crisis, how can you focus to make it personal? If you discover you have a character but no situation, what does this character want more than anything in the world? We'll discuss characters in depth in my next letter. Once you pair your idea with an individual, you can tackle even the biggest, most unwieldy concepts and make them manageable. More importantly, you'll have a story you will be invested in seeing through to the end.

Characters

Dear Writer,

Today I will discuss characters with you. All of your characters, starting with your protagonist.

For you to write believable characters, you must understand people. As a child, my father taught me how to people-watch. We would sit in a public place, such as a waiting room or a park bench, and observe those around us. My father would lean toward me and whisper, "See that guy in the striped shirt. He's going to ask that woman in a red dress on a date. She'll say yes." I would discreetly glance in their direction, waiting for the drama to unfold. My father's predictions would always manifest. The guy in the striped shirt would approach the woman in the red dress and ask her out. She would say yes. I asked my father, "How come you're always right about what strangers will do?" My father smiled. "I know how to read people. If you can read people, you'll know what they'll do." That's the power of observation. As a writer, you need to develop this skill.

In memoir, we draw upon the people we know to create our cast of characters. In fiction, we take our years of experience observing those around us to inform our made-up people.

For example, say you want your heroine to be a young, naïve, and ambitious career woman intent on making a name for herself in her chosen industry in today's world. You might recall every person you've met who meets those requirements. That is a good place to start. But you'll want to take it further and infuse your observations through your imagination. Ask questions. What would that woman look like? How would she dress and carry herself? What would she value? Who would her role models be? What about her dark side? What does she hide from others? What truth does she conceal from herself? Does she have any previous trauma? How about any childhood memories that shaped the foundation of her beliefs and values or misbeliefs and false values? What motivates her? What are her greatest fears? What are her dearest aspirations? What challenges her? What people or lack of people does she surround herself with? What is her idea of the perfect day? The perfect date? The perfect career? The perfect love? The perfect friend? The perfect family?

Drawing from your observations and imagination, you start to sketch out your protagonist. You don't need to know everything about her. Focus on the basic facts, such as name, age, occupation, and appearance. Maybe you also know her family history, her psychic wound, and her deepest secret. Maybe you don't. No worries. As you write, you make discoveries. Your protagonist likes the color yellow but hates the taste and texture of strawberry jam on toasted whole wheat bread. She likes to get up early and never stays out past midnight. Her shoulders chronically hurt from slumping before the keyboard, but the soles of her feet are smooth from weekly pedicures. She yells at her neighbors but talks sweetly to the barista at her favorite local coffee shop where she orders a triple mocha no whip on payday. The more you explore your character, the more three-dimensional your character will become.

Repeat this process with all of your major characters. Minor characters and characters who make a guest appearance do not need that much attention. Maybe a detail or two is all you need.

Be careful not to make your characters too perfect. Readers need someone they can relate to and bond with and care about. The best way to make that happen is to give your major characters flaws or weaknesses. Most writers neglect this step. They create what are called self-insert characters—people who are better versions of themselves. Everyone in the story world adores them, except the antagonist. These characters, while fun to write, make you lose credibility with readers. No one can identify with a smart, beautiful, young woman whose only challenge is to prove she is intelligent to everyone around her. Readers want to see her flaws. Maybe she is clumsy, tripping over her feet, which makes it impossible for her to wear heels. Maybe she struggles with negative self-talk from being raised by perfectionistic parents, and now she struggles to silence the internal chatter that says she is stupid. Maybe she has a scar from a childhood accident that makes her self-conscious, and she will only be intimate in the dark. Maybe she tries to hide a learning disability. Maybe she lacks impulse control around food or money. Maybe she has an annoying habit of crunching on ice chips. The point is to make her relatable and real. Good but not perfect. Frayed but not broken. Even positive traits can be spun as negatives if taken to extremes. Is your protagonist too trusting? Is she too empathetic? Remember even saints and superheroes have fatal flaws.

A question I'm often asked is, "Does my character have to be likeable?"

Depends. I wrote about a protagonist who struggled with compulsive eating, out-of-control drinking, and laziness. My editor said the protagonist wasn't likeable. "Tone her down," she said. "Make her eat less, drink only after work hours, and pick up the mess in the kitchen. It's okay to show her imperfections but don't make her beyond repair."

Other editors don't care if the protagonist is unlikeable as long as she is interesting.

But what makes for an interesting character?

Think about your favorite literary characters and the traits that made them memorable, but not likeable. In *Gone Girl*, Gillian Flynn's protagonist, Amy, isn't a nice person. She fakes her own death. But she is interesting. She has an inscrutable mind and a troubled childhood from being the inspiration for her parents' successful children's book series. Her husband, Nick, is a philanderer, but he's also charming and attentive. Unreliable narrators with streaks of anti-social behavior fascinate readers. You might not want to be friends with Nick or Amy, but you don't mind seeing what they do and how those around them react.

Now that you have a cast of interesting characters, you need to give at least the protagonist and the antagonist, if there is one, a goal that is fueled by their greatest desire. What does your protagonist want more than anything in the world? How far will she go to get it?

All of your characters will have desires. Even the barista wants to be tipped. But only your protagonist and antagonist will have goals that drive the storyline.

Once you have your cast of developed characters, you're ready to embark on plot, which is the topic we'll discuss in my next letter.

Till then, happy writing,

Angela

P.S. Characters are who they are because of everything that has happened to them up to this moment in time. Some writers refer to this state as a person's location. When you are developing characters, make sure you consider the person's location, including their current emotional state.

Do not let minor characters steal the story. If the barista is more interesting than the protagonist, give the barista her own story.

Ready to develop some characters? Try this:

1. Write a scene about your protagonist being late for an appointment. The goal is to capture their personality under pressure. How do they react? What are their instinctual or habitual responses? Are there any stakes involved in their tardiness? Aim to write between 500 and 1,000 words.
2. Place your character in an uncomfortable situation, such as a party where they know only the host or a funeral where there is family tension. Write 500 to 1,000 words showing the character interacting with others. Use action and dialogue.
3. If you're struggling with how to describe your character's appearance, write 500 to 1,000 words about how your character feels wearing their favorite item of clothing. Start by making a list of all the clothing's attributes. Use specific, sensory details grounded in sight, sound, taste, touch, or smell. Focus on how the clothing makes the character feel—powerful, loving, attentive, competent, or attractive.
4. If you want to add dimension to your protagonist, write a 500-to-1,000-word scene in which your protagonist acts out of character. Make three lists of

five things your character always does, five things your character rarely does, and five things your character never does. Now pick something from the "never" list and write *how* the surprising thing happened, *not why*. Do not explain in psychological terms. Use action, dialogue, or thoughts to show the reader. Use at least two sensory details in addition to the most common one of sight. Try to make the scene believable.

Plot

Dear Writer,

At the heart of every good plot is the question: Will the protagonist achieve her goal?

Plot is the journey leading to the answer.

If you follow the traditional Aristotelian view of story with its linear trajectory of a beginning, middle, and end, the plot can be further broken down into the elements of inciting incident, rising action, climax, and denouncement.

The inciting incident is something that barrels down the road of the protagonist's life and hits her when she least expects it, leaving a gaping hole.

The rising action is the steps she takes to fix or fill that hole in her life.

The climax is whether she succeeds or fails.

The denouncement is the final resolution, including the tying up of loose ends.

When composing my first draft, I never use this structure. Why not? Because I write to discover what the protagonist's desire is. In the second draft, I come up with the major dramatic question (Will the protagonist achieve her goal?) and revise accordingly.

Every writer comes up with their plots differently. Some prefer to outline the major events. Others like to write based on the cause and effect of the protagonist's actions and reactions. Still others combine elements of both outlining and cause and effect to come up with their own process.

If you don't know which method to use, experiment. Try plotting. An excellent book on plotting is *Save the Cat! Writes a Novel* by Jessica Brody.

If you prefer to follow the responses of the characters, then write scene by scene the way I do. One action leads to another's reaction, and the plot unfolds internally and externally.

A lot of my students worry their plots are too simplistic. Most of the time the problem isn't with the series of events but what underlies them.

For example, let's say your protagonist wants a promotion. She has been working overtime to research a project. On the day of her presentation, she oversleeps and arrives at work while the board meeting is in progress. Everyone turns and glares at her for the intrusion. Because of her tardiness, she must wait until her co-worker finishes his pitch before she begins her presentation. She fidgets, and her mind races. Can she pull this presentation off and secure her promotion? Or will she fail? She doesn't feel prepared. Or maybe she feels overprepared. Or maybe she's just exhausted. By the time her turn arrives, she's worked herself into a fluster. She stutters and forgets important facts and figures. As a result, the board eliminates funding for her project. She does not get her promotion.

This cause-and-effect series of events seems uncomplicated.

But if you dig deeper beyond the external goal, you discover the protagonist is more nuanced. She grew up in a household that demanded perfection. She could not fail without losing her parents' love and approval. For her, success is tied up with security and belonging. Failure destabilizes the foundation of her being, and she finds herself unloved and alone.

Knowing this information, you could revamp the plot to heighten the stakes, which increases the conflict and the complexity.

In my opinion, the best plots and plot twists originate internally rather than externally. That's why I prefer discovery writing. I need to learn about my characters in action to understand how they work.

You may disagree. For you, the best plots might be externally based and meticulously outlined.

It doesn't matter what method you use. What matters is you follow what works for you.

Experiment, experiment, experiment.

And have fun.

Another question I am frequently asked is, "Does the novel have to have a subplot or a parallel plot?"

No.

In fact, I advise students to focus on only one storyline. Why? It's less complicated.

A streamlined plot doesn't have to be boring.

One of my favorite student stories was about an eight-year-old girl who wanted a glass of water. As I read, I could barely swallow, my mouth was so dry. When the girl's mother yelled at her to get out of the house and wait for her father to come pick her up, I wanted to shout back, "Give me a glass of water, first." But the girl knew from experience her mother wouldn't allow for any refreshment. Her mother wanted her daughter outside, so she could avoid seeing her no-good ex-husband's face when he rolled up in his new car. By the time I finished the story, I felt a great thirst for love and understanding and forgiveness as well as a visceral need for water.

A well-executed plot doesn't need tons of twists and reversals. It must only satisfy a reader.

What else can I tell you about the behind-the-scenes mechanics of plotting?

When I teach short story writers about plot, I usually reference *The Three Little Pigs*. But that example doesn't suffice for novels. Because the landscape of a novel is so vast, the terrain is rugged, full of pit stops and side trails, layovers and distractions. Even a linear plot doesn't play out neatly, especially in a first draft. For novels, I like to refer to the plot as a mouse maze in which there is only one correct path for the mouse to obtain the cheese but there are countless dead ends. I often write until I reach a dead end. When I discover no way forward, I back up to the last scene that worked and allow the character to explore the other choices available. If that choice leads to another roadblock, I repeat the process. Eventually, I will find the only path forward.

If you prefer to map out every step of your story, please allow for detours and surprises. Sometimes characters develop a life of their own and rebel against their predetermined destiny. Don't fall into frustration or despair. Count this happenstance as a blessing. If you are surprised, a reader will be surprised.

When something doesn't work out, I always cut that section of the narrative and paste it into a new document and save it as "Notes." Sometimes my Notes document is longer than my manuscript. Who cares? I find this document a valuable resource during the revision process. Once in a while, I'll go back and copy and paste a paragraph or section into a subsequent draft. Most of the time I never revisit those Notes. But it's good to have them.

Finally, if you run into any problems and don't know what happens next, ask your protagonist. In my live classes, I often guide my students through a visualization where they go for a walk with their main character and engage them in a conversation. I ask them to listen for the answers. Once the guided visualization ends, I give them fifteen minutes to transcribe what they remember. You can do this exercise in the comfort of your home, or you can go for a walk and play the conversation in your mind as you observe your surroundings. You can repeat this exercise any time you need inspiration. Talk to your character and listen to their response. You'll be surprised by what you learn.

Now take this newfound knowledge and get writing.

All the best,

Angela

P.S. Here are a few exercises to try when you're stuck with what comes next in your novel:

1. What steps does your character need to take to achieve their goal? List the steps. Now focus on the first step and write a scene showing the character in action. Keep it simple.
2. Borrow a plot device from a different genre. For example, take the fairy-tale cliché where everything must end happily ever after. Can you apply this concept to your horror novel? Maybe it won't work for the overall story, but how about the next scene? What can the protagonist do to make herself happy in this moment?
3. Focus on conflict. Internal conflict is harder to demonstrate. Make a list of five ways your character can self-sabotage. Be as specific as

possible. For example, swap "negative self-talk" with "When someone says I can do it, I doubt myself even more." Next list five successes your character achieved despite these self-sabotages. They can be small successes. List them anyway. Finally, write a scene in which your character struggles with the temptation to self-sabotage in their journey to achieve their goal. Do they succeed or fail?
4. Finally, if you're stuck between two or more options your protagonist can take, write a 500-word scene exploring each outcome. You can even frame it as the protagonist looking back on their lives after the events and ruminating on their regrets about the roads not taken. Make each situation and outcome concrete. Then, examine which outcome works best for the story you wish to write.

Final tip: Sometimes all the pieces fall into place if you let them. Never force your outline on your characters or your story will feel stiff or artificial.

Psychological Barriers

Dear Writer,

    I didn't want to write to you today.
Why?
I ran into some resistance.
I know you've felt the same way.
    For a distraction, I left the keyboard and prepared dinner for my disabled son. He's almost thirty and functions more like a toddler. I didn't mind cooking for him, but no one slaves away in the kitchen at two o'clock in the afternoon for a simple dinner that will be served four hours later.
    While waiting for the water to boil, I confessed to my husband that I should be writing.
    "Everyone needs a break," he said.
    "But I haven't started." I could hear the whiny tone in my voice. "I turned all those notes I have for my students on how to write a novel into a book of letters. The manuscript is complete in longhand. I only need to type it into the computer, but I am running into resistance."
    "Wait." He frowned. "You've written a book about writing a book?"

I nodded. The way he phrased it sounded trite and silly.

I started looking for ways to push through resistance. First, I thought about sending an email to Nicole. She's a writer who teaches. But she didn't write about teaching.

Next, I thought of calling Andrea. Typically, we meet once a month and edit each other's stories. Neither one of us has sought advice from the other in terms of craft or motivation. We're more inclined to discuss our personal lives.

That's when I realized I needed to write to you.

You are the only one who understands.

That fear of success. That fear of failure. It cripples you. It paralyzes all thought and creativity.

Every idea sounds ridiculous.

Every character comes across as a stereotype.

Why am I trying to tell a story when every story has already been told?

When I look at my written thoughts to you, I realize I'm doing exactly what I tell my students not to do.

I'm doubting myself.

I'm doubting my writing.

I've fallen victim to imposter syndrome.

Yes, even professional authors suffer from this ailment where every word choice, every craft skill, every story idea is questioned and discarded. Self-esteem plummets to an all-time low. You think of giving up writing and adopting a safer hobby like needlepoint. You scrub the tiles in the shower stall with an old toothbrush because the grout is dirty. You haul off all the clothes you haven't worn in one year to the secondhand store. You volunteer for every activity you can find. You do everything in your power to avoid confronting the ugly truth about yourself—you don't believe in yourself and your story, but you can't abandon the fantasy of having written or the hopes of reaching readers someday. Caught in a conundrum, you toggle back and forth between starting and stopping. Your novel never gets finished, and you end up becoming a statistic, which proves your theory that you aren't good enough and your story wasn't original enough, and what gave you the grandiose idea that you could be the next J.K. Rowling anyway?

Extreme thinking? Perhaps. But most of us writers suffer from it occasionally.

How do you overcome this resistance?

You stop comparing yourself to other writers. You focus on what you've accomplished instead of what you hope to achieve. You cling to the fiery energy of your original concept and push forward one word at a time. Maybe you set a timer and write freehand for five minutes. Maybe you promise yourself a slice of chocolate cake if you write one scene or 500 words. Maybe you pause to consider why you are avoiding writing. Do you have a doubt or fear you need to confront? Is this story not enough to sustain you through the ups and downs of writing through the fog?

Whatever it is, you need to deal with it.

If you don't, you'll end up regretting your decision to abandon a lifelong dream. You may end up walking away anyway, if you determine this novel-writing gig isn't what your heart truly desires. But unless you take a moment to examine your resistance, you will never know the truth.

So, why did I resist writing to you today?

I went online and searched for books on writing. Tons of them popped up, from how to outline your novel in a day to how to write your first draft in 10 days. A lot of those books were written by authors you would recognize by name. They are the ones who constantly make the bestseller list or have their stories turned into movies. Who am I to think my bundle of homemade letters will make an impact on anyone who desires to write a novel? What do I have to contribute to the thousands of books already written about craft or motivation?

Actually, if you ask my former students, I have a wealth of information and experience to offer.

Hundreds of people can't all be wrong, can they?

Maybe they can.

Most likely a handful of them are right.

What if out of that handful of students, one of them goes on to write a novel that becomes a classic someday? What if that student would have given up on their first draft if they had not attended my class and applied my advice?

What if one of you reading this letter has the potential to write a life-changing story but you've run into so many obstacles, you're ready to quit? What if this letter inspires you to continue writing?

If I can reach just one writer and offer them the encouragement needed to finish the first draft, then I've succeeded in my goal.

But if I give up and refuse to type a manuscript that has already been written because I am daunted by the overwhelming fear of failure and my own insecurities as a writer and an instructor, then I will never reach the one person who needs to read these words.

You.

Now, go write.

Till next time,

Angela

P.S. What are your psychological barriers?

Do you have an editor perched on your shoulder critiquing every word you write? Banish her until the second draft.

Do you keep comparing yourself to your favorite author? Stop reading that author's work (or any work) while drafting your novel.

Do you struggle with excuses? Dig deep. What do those excuses mask? Everyone has doubts and insecurities. Even famous, bestselling authors have bad writing days. Some of their novels even fail. Examine your relationship with success and failure. How have they shaped your life?

If you feel resistance to writing and you can't name what's lying underneath, take a walk. Luxuriate in your surroundings. Sometimes when we are still, the answers surface. Let them come to you. Once you identify the problem, you can apply some of the techniques discussed in this letter.

When nothing works, remember to cultivate a kind, loving, and encouraging inner voice. Practice becoming your own best friend. Place one hand on your heart and one on your belly. Close your eyes and take a deep breath. What advice would you give your best friend now?

Your Story's Universe

Dear Writer,

Today I want to discuss setting *and* world building. Both are important.

Setting is a specific time and place. Often setting is one of the first elements of a scene. Readers need to know where the action is taking place: a hotel room or a bar, a park or a stadium, a bathroom or a closet.

On the other hand, world building is all encompassing. It is the culmination of every location visited by your cast of characters for the duration of the novel. Often it helps to develop this universe before placing any of your characters on the page. Why? Because a protagonist needs to know their environment before they can determine what course of action to take, which ties in directly with plot. Is this world friendly or hostile? Familiar or unknown? Claustrophobic or comfy? Expansive with possibilities or contractive with restrictions? By defining your protagonist's world, you set the stage for the drama to unfold. This environment can either support or hinder your protagonist from achieving their goal. A loving and generous world will support your character. A hostile and uncaring world will not. In this way, your story's universe will influence the story's mood, theme, and conflicts.

Think about some classic storylines such as man versus nature. In *Moby Dick* by Herman Melville, Captain Ahab seeks to destroy the albino sperm whale that made him a cripple. Melville's universe encompasses the dangerous and unpredictable world of whaling in the nineteenth century. This precarious environment escalates Ahab's obsession for revenge at the cost of his crew's safety. On the other hand, *Jaws* by Peter Benchley takes place in a small tourist town at the height of summer in the twentieth century. This carefree and relaxed environment is underscored by the threat of sharks—the perfect backdrop for a thriller.

How do you know you've discovered the ideal setting? Easy. The story could not take place anywhere else.

For example, Gabriel Garcia Marquez's *One Hundred Years of Solitude* wouldn't work in the twenty-first century. There are too many distractions (TVs, computers, cell phones) competing with the world's magical realism.

Sophie Kinsella's *Confessions of a Shopaholic* relies heavily on consumerism. Placing the story in a monastery or a third world country destroys the story's premise of how a young businesswoman drowning in debt can rise above her compulsive spending and take charge of her life.

Where *must* your story take place?

It's okay if you don't know.

Here are some things to consider:

Genre: A post-apocalyptic world (sci-fi and fantasy) is different than a small western town (historical and westerns), but a small western town can be set in a post-apocalyptic world (sci-fi western).

Culture: Paris, France, has different customs and values than Cairo, Egypt.

Weather: Miami, Florida, evokes humid weather and warm water while Anchorage, Alaska, summons long, dark nights and plenty of snow.

Furthermore, people are shaped by their surroundings as much as they are by their families and personal histories. When setting and world building are thought of this way, location is everything.

Once you decide on your world, how do you create it?

Through carefully chosen details woven in through characters and action. Avoid dumping paragraphs of setting onto the page. Often just a sentence or two are needed to orient both characters and readers.

Additionally, you want to ground your world in the five senses—sight, sound, taste, touch, and smell. You also need to add the components that make up your world—street names, businesses, and neighborhoods. All these effects will be filtered through your point-of-view narrator, which we will discuss in the next letter. For now, it is enough to know where your story takes place.

Sometimes we don't know enough details to create the setting. That's where research comes into play. If you can't afford to go to a location, then study maps or talk to people who live in the area. If your setting is entirely fabricated, such as a planet in a distant galaxy, take the time to draw a map and write down notes about its atmosphere, history, values, and customs. Even if you're writing about your current city, you owe it to your readers to get the facts right. Verify anything and everything to make the world as believable as possible. You may not use all your research, but writing from a place of knowledge will imbue your words with strength and power.

But don't let research stop you from writing. Mark the manuscript with an asterisk and note what details need to be filled in later. You only need to know enough about your world to begin writing now.

More later,

Angela

P.S. Here are some ideas to explore when coming up with setting:

1. Write 500–1,000 words about a time your character wanted to go home or returned home after some time away. Use sensory details.
2. Map out your character's world. Start with the physical location, then expand to include imaginary borders, such as cultural and racial divides within neighborhoods.
3. Place your character in a season—spring, summer, fall, or winter. Write 500 words showing your character in the middle of a work or personal obligation and how the weather affects their ability to complete their task.
4. Imagine your character in an uncomfortable setting that brings up a lot of dread, such as a dental office. Show the character moving through this space and how they feel through their body language.

Point of View and Voice

Dear Writer,

Before we get too far into your first draft, let's talk about how to choose which point of view and tense to use and how to develop your writing voice.

I know what you're thinking. I can't write in the first person. I only know my own voice, and I don't want my character to sound like me.

I also don't want to write in the second person. Who reads books addressed to "you" anyway?

And don't get me started on the omniscient point of view. I don't believe in a god, so why would I write from that perspective?

Well, you have good reasons for your objections, but you've narrowed your options to third person distant, third person close, and the objective, which I don't recommend if you're trying to connect with the reader.

While I don't talk too much about publishing during the first draft, I do mention it here because I know from experience that point of view and voice can sell your novel. When I wrote *Just Juliet*, I couldn't find a publisher for the rom-com because first-person present-tense stories had fallen out of favor. If I had been reading *Publishers Weekly* or paying attention to the books entering the market, I would have realized this fact. But I was too busy composing my story to bother. I revised and resubmitted the novel in the third-person past tense, but the editor passed. If you're writing to sell, I suggest looking at the current trends of both the books being purchased and debuting today. The typical time it takes from signed contract to book tour is twelve-to-eighteen months. The typical life cycle of a certain point of view and verb tense is five years. With this general information, you can determine what perspective to choose before you start writing.

If you don't care about publishing trends, then you need to look at the story you wish to tell.

Here are some benefits and drawbacks for each of your options:

The first-person point of view creates instant intimacy with the reader. The narrator is embodied in the story, and the reader witnesses everything through the narrator's perspective. The voice is the narrator's voice, so word choice and diction reflect the character's personality and level of education. A blue-collar worker with a high school diploma speaks differently than a white-collar worker with a college diploma. My first memoir, *Red Eggs and Good Luck*, was written from this perspective. Since I write my memoirs using the same techniques I use for fiction, I feel this example is valid.

The second-person point of view addresses the reader directly. "You" may be offensive to some readers but inviting to others. Whenever I choose this perspective, I think of the reader as the beloved. This prevents me from alienating the reader by involving them directly in the story and creates a level of trust and intimacy by allowing the reader to be part of the experience. *The Fool and the*

Magician, my second memoir, was written from this perspective.

The omniscient point of view allows the reader to witness everything all at once. The omniscient narrator can tell us what is happening both externally and internally from every character's experience no matter where those characters may be. Celeste Ng uses this perspective in her novel *Everything I Never Told You*.

The objective point of view is similar to the perspective of a journalist who is *not* part of the story. The reader only gets the facts without the emotional resonance that lies beyond the surface. I don't know any novels that employ this perspective, but Shirley Jackson's short story "The Lottery" does.

The third-person distant perspective allows an unnamed narrator to tell the story. It's almost like the objective point of view, but it typically shadows one character, usually the protagonist, from beginning to end. In that sense, the reader gets to witness things from this person's perspective but only at a distance. Think of it as viewing the story through a camera attached to the protagonist's head.

On the other hand, the third-person close point of view allows the reader a similar intimacy experienced through the first-person perspective. Unlike first person where you are limited by the narrator's personality and education, third-person close allows you to use your own language to describe the narrative. Additionally, you get to experience the story from inside your protagonist's body. You are privy to the thoughts and physical sensations of the protagonist. This technique allows you to *both* become the protagonist *and* maintain the autonomy of your creative writing skill set. You can use flowery language your protagonist wouldn't use while describing the protagonist's experience of the story from the inside out.

So, if you insist on using the third person, which option do you choose: distant or close?

Personally, I suggest trying them out by writing a scene in both perspectives. Which one feels more natural to you? Which one allows you to share the version of the story you wish the reader to experience?

After you decide on point of view, you need to determine your voice. A lot of times instructors will say you can't teach voice. A writer develops their voice only after years of practice. Don't believe it. You can alter your written voice just as easily as you can modify your speaking voice.

Again, go back to the experience you want to create for the reader. A formal voice will keep the reader at a distance. An informal voice will pull the reader a little closer. A conversational voice will make the reader your best friend. On the other hand, a journalistic voice will be in keeping with that objective perspective, allowing the reader to come to their own conclusions. A lyrical voice will mimic the sound of music, giving the reader a poetic or elevated experience.

If you don't know, write a scene in each of the voices until you find one you can sustain for the long haul.

Voice does develop with skill and practice. But I think voice comes from a writer's level of confidence. If you go boldly into writing your story, that command of language will come across in your voice. If you are hesitant and full of doubt, that also will show in your voice.

Feel free to experiment and play around with both the point of view and voice until you find the right fit for this particular story.

In my opinion, it's better to write in a natural-sounding voice and perspective that breaks genre conventions and defies publishing expectations than it is to write in a voice and perspective that sounds formulaic or boring. If the perspective energizes and engages you while writing, it will most likely energize and engage the reader.

Before I go, let me mention something about verb tenses.

If your story involves a lot of reflection, you want to use past tense. This technique allows for the characters, especially the point-of-view character, the time and distance to process the action and impart wisdom to the audience.

On the other hand, if you want the reader to experience the events at the same time as the protagonist, choose the present tense. Nothing beats the immediacy.

Whatever tense you choose, be consistent. Nothing takes a reader out of a story quicker than flipping back and forth between past and present tense at inappropriate moments.

Ready?

Go ahead. Try out those different points of view, voices, and tenses. Discover what works for you and your story.

Happy writing,

Angela

P.S. Still stymied?

Here's my favorite exercise to give students when studying point of view:

Write a scene about a dognapping at an apartment complex from the first person, third person close or distant, and omniscient points of view. You can choose either a different character for each point of view or the same one. You can also vary the tense, choosing past or present. Mix it up. See which one feels more natural and which one feels the most challenging. Then try it out in your novel.

Here are my versions for your reference (I chose the past tense for each of these examples):

<u>First person, Clara's point of view</u>:

When Rodrigo approached the front desk of the leasing office dressed in a rumpled T-shirt, sweats, and loafers with his hair stuck up on end, I gasped.

"I need your help," Rodrigo said, clutching a pink diamond-studded dog collar and leash.

Standing abruptly, I banged the office chair against the wall and teetered on my new heels. My heart banged inside my chest. "Where's Fiona?" I loved that adorable pug-and-chihuahua-mix princess. Was she lost?

Rodrigo led me to the dog park. The gate was flung open, and a woman lay facedown in the tanbark. The back of my neck prickled with goose bumps even though the morning heat hinted at record highs today. For a moment, I racked my brain, searching for the name of Fiona's owner.

"Did you call an ambulance?" I asked.

Rodrigo nodded, his fist still clutching the leash.

I couldn't tell if the woman was unconscious or dead. Glancing around, I didn't notice anything that would have made her fall. I scanned the perimeter one more time. That's when I noticed the missing security camera. Damn it, someone probably dognapped Fiona, and stole the video that proved it.

<u>Third person close, Rodrigo's point of view</u>:

"Where's Fiona?" Clara asked when he ran up to her desk in the lobby of Glenmore Garden Apartments with the dog's leash in his hand.

"I need your help," Rodrigo said. The air conditioner chilled his flushed skin, and he trembled. "Out in the dog park."

Clara stumbled from behind her desk on those ridiculous heels she always wore. Who saw her feet anyway? Rodrigo shook his head, waiting those painfully long seconds for her dainty feet to catch up with him. Why did he bother telling her about Mrs. Stiles anyway? She didn't kneel and take her pulse like he did. She only asked if he had called an ambulance. Yes, he already had. She glanced around the perimeter of the yard, scowling until she noticed the cut wires where the security camera had been.

Rodrigo's grip slackened and the leash dropped into a coil on the tanbark. Fiona hadn't run away. She had been dognapped. Without the video tape, she probably wouldn't be found.

Omniscient point of view:

Rodrigo jolted awake at the sound of a woman screaming followed by a dog barking and tires squealing until a hollow silence rang in his head. Jumping up, he shoved his feet into a pair of loafers and jogged outside. The morning sunlight crashed against his face, and he squinted at the creaking gate of the dog park. Something glittered in the tanbark. As he approached, the object took shape. He gulped. Mrs. Stiles in Apartment 309 lay facedown next to Fiona's leash.

When Rodrigo came to get her, Clara didn't know what to expect. She had been working at Glenmore Garden Apartments for only six weeks as the leasing manager, and she didn't know all the tenants yet, only their pets. She didn't recognize Mrs. Stiles lying facedown in the tanbark of the dog park, but she did notice the missing security camera. She shook her head and tapped her stilettoed feet. Another crime. The second one this week.

Dialogue

Dear Writer,

I hear your concerns. You're not sure how to capture a conversation or when to show versus when to tell.

I don't want to overwhelm you, so I will tackle each in a separate letter.

This one will focus on dialogue.

You have a lot of options about how to write and convey dialogue. Traditionally, dialogue is written within quotes and includes a tag to show the reader who is speaking.

"Is this how it looks to write dialogue?" you ask.

Yes, that's exactly right.

But you're not limited to writing dialogue with quotes.

You can delete them altogether.

Or you can summarize speech, so it's included in the narrative.

Why are there so many options?

Because language is constantly evolving, which means literature is, too.

If you don't know how you want to write dialogue, I suggest you study your favorite authors. What techniques do they use?

Here are some general guidelines to get you started:

First, dialogue should convey the character's personality. Everyone speaks differently. Maybe one character has a pet phrase she uses. Geraldine Jones in the *Women of the Crush* trilogy calls everyone "sugar." Maybe your character has a lisp or stutters or repeats herself.

Second, dialogue should move the story forward or reveal character. How someone says something is just as important as what that person says. Conflict and tension often flow through spoken words. Let your characters battle it out through dialogue.

Third, dialogue should sound natural and mimic real-life speech without being a transcript. You don't want to clutter your dialogue with a lot of "umms" and "huhs" and "mm-hmms" even if that's how your characters talk. Same with greetings. We don't need to see every, "Hi, how are you?" and "Good to meet you" every time a new character is introduced. What you do want to capture is the heart of the matter. Is your protagonist angry with her husband? Let us hear what she says.

Your protagonist may be cagey. People don't always say what they mean, but they hint at it. This technique is called subtext.

A great example of subtext is Ernest Hemingway's "Hills Like White Elephants." In the short story, which is mostly dialogue, a couple sits at a bar discussing the scenery, but they're really talking about the woman's unplanned pregnancy and possible abortion.

Not every story has subtext, and not every person uses it. But it is a good technique to have in your writer's toolbox.

Fourth, you can replace some dialogue tags with action tags. You can also delete the tags altogether if it is clear to the reader who is speaking.

In my paranormal romance, *Blood Moon Rising*, Valkyrie, a vampire, and her dhampir son, Anthony, have traveled from the forest to the city to locate Anthony's father, from whom he needs his blood. In the hotel room, Valkyrie and Anthony have a verbal exchange in the bathroom while Anthony soaks in the tub.

Here's an excerpt of the dialogue:

> Anthony soaked in the shallow tub with the water up to his waist just above his lower ribs. "This is no fun," he whined. "I want to swim in the pool."
> Valkyrie sat on the toilet seat and stared at the absence of her reflection in the mirror. "You heard your friend. You can't."
> "During the day I can."
> "You sleep during the day."
> "I don't have to. I can learn to sleep at night."
> "You have to stay with me."
> "Then come swimming with me. We'll make lots of friends."
> "I can't. I'm allergic to sunlight." Valkyrie rubbed her temples.

In the example, once it is established who is speaking, the reader understands the conversation toggles back and forth between the two characters each time a new paragraph starts.

Also, in that example, the characters are not static. Anthony fills the tub and soaks in the water. Valkyrie sits on the toilet and rubs her temples. Action takes place during the conversation.

Finally, you have the option of summarizing dialogue if the content is more important than the delivery. The following example is from *The Last White Man* by Mohsin Hahid. In this excerpt, the two protagonists, Anders and Oona, are taking a walk during this summarized conversation.

> …Anders said that he was not sure he was the same person, he had begun by feeling that under the surface it was still him, who else could it be, but it was not that simple, and the way people act around you, it changes what you are, who you are, and Oona said she understood, that it was like learning a foreign language…

    Hahid prefers to keep his signature style of writing one long, languid paragraph-length sentence during this exchange. Because of this decision, he does not quote the protagonists directly.
    The best way to learn dialogue is by examining the conversations in your favorite novels. Read them aloud. Listen to the cadence of the words. Note any hints of dialect, slang, or phrases that make the speaker unique. If you want, you can write down those lines in a notebook.
    Some writers listen to audio books to master dialogue. I haven't tried this technique, so I can't vouch for it. But it is another option.
    My father, who was a great storyteller, spent time eavesdropping. Whenever he was in public, he would listen intently to the conversations taking place around him. If I was with him, he would tell me who these people were by what they said and how they said it. Go ahead and try it. Take a notebook with you to a café. Sit behind a table where a conversation is happening. Write down everything you hear. Then, the next day, take that transcription and shape it into dialogue. Make each character distinguishable only through what they say.

Writing dialogue, like any skill, takes time to develop.

Now go practice,

Angela

P.S. Do you need more ideas on how to develop your ear for dialogue?

Place your protagonist on the phone with another character. Record just the protagonist's half of the conversation. Pay attention to how your protagonist speaks. What words do they use. What do they include in the conversation, and what do they leave out. Make it sound real.

Create a dialogue around a misunderstanding between two characters. Maybe someone forgot to do something. Or maybe someone misheard directions. Do your best to capture not only the conversation but the feelings behind the spoken words.

Chapters, Scenes, and Summaries

Dear Writer,

Today we'll cover when to show and when to tell when writing your first draft. We'll break these elements down into chapters, scenes, and summaries.

How many chapters are in a typical novel? I suggest checking with recently published books in the genre you're writing.

Additionally, some publishers, such as The Wild Rose Press, have detailed guidelines for chapter word count. Others don't.

Typically, a chapter consists of one or more scenes. When I write romance, my chapters consist of two scenes—one from the point of view of the male protagonist and another from the point of view of the female protagonist. My novels typically comprise between thirty and forty chapters. So, if I write a scene a day, and two scenes equal one chapter, and my novel is thirty-five chapters, I will have a first draft completed in seventy days or two and a half months.

But don't model your writing pace or your number of chapters on what I do. Everyone and every story are different. You need to discover what works for you and your story.

Now let's move on to writing scenes. A scene is something that happens at a specific place and specific time. Think of it as living in the moment. When you think about something in the past (flashback or memory) or dwell on something in the future (planning or strategizing), you're not experiencing this moment (scene).

Scenes are mini stories in the sense that they have a narrative arc with a beginning, middle, and end. The beginning introduces the goal of the scene. The middle shows the conflict escalating. The end resolves the current conflict. Either the goal is achieved, not achieved, or deferred or evolved. Most importantly, a new challenge is introduced that propels the plot forward.

A scene is where you "show" a reader what is happening. You slow down and let the reader experience every relevant physical sensation through your point-of-view character using as many of the five senses as possible. When you're in doubt about how much detail to use, always return to your narrator's perspective. What would she notice? For example, someone who cares about fashion might know the clothing brands the other characters are wearing. Name them. Someone who has a sensitive nose will notice smells. Name them. Someone who is deaf in one ear might not hear what's going on around them. Let the information ebb and flow depending on whether the sound is traveling toward their good ear or their bad ear. Someone who doesn't like how slippery satin feels will complain about the texture. The deeper you know your point-of-view character, the easier it is to write a scene.

Depending on the scene, you might have one or more characters acting or talking or reflecting.

Now, you ask, "Where do I tell?"

Easy. Most novels are sixty to ninety percent of scenes. In the space where the action is not shown is where the story is told—the other ten to forty percent.

Typically, a novel weaves back and forth between scene and summary. Summary is where you tell the reader what happened between the scenes: the protagonist went home, slept ten hours, ate breakfast, and drove to work. The next scene shows the protagonist at work.

Another area where you might rely on telling is backstory or exposition. Whatever happened before the novel opened may or may not be relevant. Those bits of information that the reader needs to know about a character's history to understand the current conflict are typically told in a sentence or a paragraph as needed. You never want to dump three pages of personal history into an ongoing scene. Some writers get around this problem by dramatizing the personal history through a flashback or memory where the reader gets to experience what happened in real time. When employing this technique be sure to transition the reader into and out of the flashback or memory so the reader doesn't get confused. A confused reader is someone who gets frustrated or, worse, stops reading.

Finally, don't worry too much about the balance of showing versus telling. Do whatever comes naturally to you. Once the first draft is finished, you can go back and clean up the language, either cutting or expanding as needed. Right now, you just need to keep writing till you reach the end.

Till next time,

Angela

P.S. Let's practice writing a scene. First, state the objective or obstacle in one sentence. This one-liner is for your information only. It is not part of the scene. Next, dramatize the moment through the characters' actions, dialogue, and setting. Aim for 500–1,000 words.

If you need more assistance, grab a novel off your bookshelf or check one out of the library. Read until you get to a scene. Dissect the scene by its elements. What is the objective? Who are the characters and what is the obstacle? How does the conflict escalate within this setting? What is the outcome? Does the scene end with another question?

Now look for the areas where the author has summarized information. Study how and when the technique of telling is used. If you own the book, you might want to use two different colored highlighters to differentiate between "showing/scene" and "telling/summary." This technique will give you a visual roadmap on how this particular author balances the amount of dramatization against summation.

For more step-by-step guidance with detailed examples, consider reading *Make a Scene: Crafting a Powerful Story One Scene at a Time* by Jordan E. Rosenfeld.

Opening Lines

Dear Writer,

Now you're ready to put things together and write the beginning of your novel.

Scared?

Don't be.

Some writers fret over the opening lines. They feel it is crucial to capture the reader's attention.

Other writers worry more about the end. They want to make sure the reader leaves feeling satisfied.

While both the beginning and the ending are important, they serve different purposes.

A good beginning hooks the reader into buying this novel.

A good ending convinces the reader to buy your next novel.

What goes into a good beginning?

The simplest technique is often the most effective. You can start with a sentence that includes the following elements:

Protagonist + Action + Setting = Opening Line

You say you don't like formulas. You want to be original.

Okay, here's another option.

Open with an image.

Or a line of dialogue.

Whatever you choose, you must be intrigued by it.

If you're at a loss, you can always pick up your favorite novels and read the first sentence.

Here's the opening line from *Maggie Finds Her Muse* by Dee Ernst (a great novel if you want to experience first draft angst):

Here lies Maggie Bliss, who died a slow and tortured death by total imposter syndrome after failing to write the final book of the Delania Trilogy.

This sentence gives the reader three things: the name of the protagonist, the central conflict, and the emotional consequences.

Here's the first sentence from *After I Do* by Taylor Jenkins Reid:

We are in the parking lot of Dodger Stadium, and once again, Ryan has forgotten where we left the car.

The reader knows this is a long-term couple with long-standing, unresolved issues. You can feel the tension.

Here's the first line in the satirical romantic horror novel *Patricia Wants to Cuddle* by Samantha Allen:

Margaret Davies scrubs and scrubs but she knows she'll just have to refinish the deck.

This opening sentence evokes suspense. Something has happened, and it's not easily fixed.

Finally, here's the opening sentence in Brenda Novak's romantic suspense *The Perfect Couple*:

The bump that came from the trunk of her car surprised Tiffany so much it nearly sent her careening off the road and into one of the many houses along the right side.

Immediately, the reader asks, "What's in her trunk?" and keeps reading to find out.

In writing the first draft of your novel, you don't need to be so concerned about the beginning. Often, even for experienced novelists, the true start of the novel happens scenes or chapters later. I once critiqued a student's story in which the first sentence didn't appear until 150 pages into the manuscript.
Now you're shuddering with fear.
Don't.
Stop worrying about worst-case scenarios.
Once you have the first draft, you can fix anything.
Anything.
Especially the first sentence.
Every now and then, I do have a student who can't write the rest of the book without nailing that opening line. If that's you, go ahead and fret over it until you deem it's perfect. Then proceed in earnest.
If you're like most of us, you just need to start where you feel the story begins.
When I wrote *Legs*, my first published novel, I began by imagining my first-person protagonist running on the

treadmill when she receives more bad news about her failing real estate business during the Great Recession:

"What?" I punch the pause button on the treadmill and slow to a stop, the cell phone pressed against my ear.

I chose this opening dialogue to show the protagonist's emotional reaction at the start of her day in the comfort of her at-home gym. Because I was writing chick lit, I chose the first-person present tense to create both intimacy and immediacy.

Go ahead and write five opening lines. Try one with dialogue, another with setting, one with the major conflict, another with theme, and finally one with action.

Set the sentences aside overnight. In the morning, read each sentence aloud. Which one grabs your attention? Which one begs you to ask, "And then what happened?" Pick the sentence that holds the most energy, that sizzles with potential, then write a paragraph to follow that opening line. If you feel that paragraph is solid, then write another one. And another one. Capture one scene. If you feel inspired and have the time, write another scene.

Congratulations!
You've written your beginning.

Keep on keeping on,

Angela

P.S. If for some reason your beginning fizzles out, go back and write a new opening sentence. Keep trying out first lines until you discover one that offers something to the reader that you can deliver.

Another technique you can use is to write down the first sentence of your favorite novel. Now take the sentence structure and replace it with your own words.

For example, the opening line of *The Heroic Adventures of Madame X* by A. R. Gross is:

Thirty-eight-year-old Finnegan Yates slouched over the drafting table in the oppressive summer heat of Zanesville, Ohio.

Your sentence with your protagonist acting in your setting might read:

Twenty-two-year-old Maria Santos hugged her psychology books against her chest as she hustled across Saddleback College in balmy Mission Viejo, California.

Pacing

Dear Writer,

Now that you've begun, we need to discuss pacing.

Pacing is the technique of slowing down or speeding up time.

Generally, you want to speed up time whenever nothing important is happening. Here's an example from *Last Chance*:

> An hour later, Lian almost drove past the inn.

The reader doesn't need to know the details of what occurred during that hour of time.

A scene is where you slow down time. Depending on what is happening and how important it is, you may take the reader through each moment, lingering on both the external action and internal reactions of your point-of-view narrator or you may pick up the pace by showing only what is needed as you move along the timeline.

Here's an example of slowing down time from *Last Chance*:

> After climbing the stone steps to the pink mansion, Lian froze on the landing. Strong words from a man's low voice and a woman's shrill cry battered her ears. She crouched, peering through the frosted glass of the front door. Should she leave? Glancing around at the calla lilies blooming in pots and the ivy trailing up the side of the faded blush stucco, she tried to imagine where she might hide until the danger passed. Was there a hidden entry to the courtyard?
> A lull of silence lured her. With trembling fingers, she punched the keycode into the pad. The door unlocked, and she stepped inside. A warm scent of spicy tomatoes enveloped her. She ducked into the lobby, carrying her shopping bags, and shut the door.
> From the library, the voices rose again.

In this example, the reader experiences Lian's apprehension when she approaches the inn. Voices are heard. Then silence. When Lian steps inside, she smells spicy tomatoes and hears voices again.

If we wanted to speed up time with this passage, we could write:

> Lian approached the inn but didn't enter until the shouting voices inside died down.

The more important the scene, the more you want to slow down the action. Think of the big moments in your novel: the inciting incident, the major turning point, the climax.

There is another technique, which I call "negative space," that you can use if you do not want to show the big moments.

Instead of changing the pacing, you omit these scenes completely from the novel. Stephen McCauley masters this technique in his novel *My Ex-Life*. When the teenage girl decides to work part-time for an older guy who runs both a computer repair business and a cybersex operation out of his basement, McCauley ends the scene as the teenage girl descends the stairs after her new employer tells her she can stop performing anytime she wants. She just needs to talk about the weather, and he'll come downstairs and pause the webcam. McCauley does not show the teenage girl engaged in her new job as a sex worker. Instead, he cuts to a scene with her mother, later that night, after the daughter has returned home from her first day at work. Her mother thinks her daughter is still working retail, not knowing she was fired and has taken the sex job. During the scene, as mother and daughter watch the news, the daughter cries during the weather report. This aftereffect of the omitted major turning point is enough for the reader to fill in the blanks about what happened. McCauley chooses this technique because it's more important how things affect his characters than what they do—reaction versus action.

You may or may not want to use this technique in your own writing. Personally, I find it satisfying to dive deep into the conflicts of those major battle scenes instead of lingering on the aftereffects. If you're not sure, you might experiment with writing both and seeing which one works best for you—focusing on the drama or the aftermath.

The choice is yours.

Happy writing,

Angela

P.S. Here are a couple of exercises to practice pacing:

1. Place your character in a setting in which they feel uncomfortable. It can be anywhere in your novel's universe—a dentist's chair, a job interview, a first date at a coffee shop. Describe ninety seconds of your character's experience. Focus on their thoughts, actions, and bodily sensations. Here's an added challenge—your character knows this ordeal will be over soon, so you can hint at the sense of relief coming in the future. Aim for 500 words.
2. Now condense that scene into a sentence or two or no longer than one paragraph to speed up the pacing.

Final tip: You can repeat this exercise with different increments of time: one hour, one day, one week, etc. With practice, you will learn how to manage time effectively throughout your novel.

Procrastination

Dear Writer,

    Today I didn't want to write to you.
    I pulled out all the distractions.
    I moved "write daily letter" to the bottom of my to-do list.
    Then I made it optional.
    After crossing off the previous items, I glanced at the clock. Sixty minutes until I called it a day.
    Grabbing my notebook, I sat at my desk and opened a blank page.
    Forty minutes later, I caught myself scrolling through my phone.
    The empty sheet of lined paper stared at me.
    Okay.
    Deep breath.
    I gave myself a pep talk: *You can push through this resistance. Why are you fearful of writing a letter? What's the worst thing that can happen? No one reads the letter. So what? You didn't harm anyone. No one died. What's the best thing that can happen? Someone reads the letter and is touched by it. That reader goes on to find the motivation*

needed to continue writing the first draft of their novel. That's impressive, isn't it? Just one person. Okay. Now, what do you want to say to this person?

I set the timer for twenty minutes and started writing exactly what I wanted to say to you. I started at the beginning, detailing my resistance, and ended with encouragement.

During the draft, I stopped myself from crossing out words or phrases. I kept my hand moving. If something needed to be addressed on a revision, I made an asterisk and continued writing.

In eighteen minutes, I finished the first draft.

I smiled. Two minutes to spare. Not bad. Huh?

Well, the writing would not have happened if I hadn't taken my own advice.

The best part of this process is how wonderful I felt for having written. That feeling is as good as a runner's high or a relaxing bath or winning a prize. Pure bliss. Plus, I felt productive for accomplishing everything on my to-do list.

So, have you written today? If not, what's stopping you? You, too, can write through the resistance.

All the best,

Angela

P.S. If you're struggling with procrastination, try this:

1. Get out your notebook and a pen.
2. Set your timer for five minutes.
3. Write your protagonist a to-do list.
4. Then pick two items on the to-do list for your protagonist to complete.

5. Show your protagonist working on one item when another character steps into the scene to give them something else to complete.
6. Let your character battle out how to get both things done before the scene ends.

By putting a little pressure on your character, you reveal a little bit more about who they are, what they value, and how they manage their time under stress.

You can also try this exercise on yourself. Maybe you'll discover something you didn't know about who you are, what you value, and how you manage your time under stress.

Getting through the Muddy Middle

Dear Writer,

By now, you're approaching the middle of your novel or you're already there.

Some writers, like me, dread the middle. I find it so much easier to start a story or end a story than build the conflict and compound the obstacles. Why? Because the tension needed to constantly raise the stakes creates an equal amount of stress in my writing life. How far can I push my protagonist before they crack or succumb to defeat?

First, let's go over what generally must happen in the middle of your novel:

Rising conflict— The obstacles keep coming, big and small, some so overpowering they seem insurmountable. You want to put your protagonist through hell.

Rising desire— Because the obstacles are so relentless, the protagonist must be equally relentless in their desire to fight through them. The desire must grow stronger, become all-consuming.

Rising stakes—Every now and then, a turn of events should raise the stakes, giving the protagonist more to lose or more to win.

Rising tension—If you keep those other things rising, we will feel the tension escalating, turning so tense, something needs to break.

Ideally, most of your plot is a chain of cause and effect, as opposed to a bunch of random happenings. For each action taken by your protagonist, there is a direct reaction. An obstacle arises in the character's path, your protagonist takes action to overcome it, and one of two things will happen: she will move forward, or another obstacle will rise as a result.

One way to look at novel writing is to see each event as a doorway the protagonist enters. Once that threshold is crossed, the door closes. The protagonist can't go backward, only forward. This momentum propels the narrative.

But what happens if you get stuck?

You brainstorm.

Emma Coates of Pixar suggests listing ten possibilities from which your protagonist must choose. Why ten? Because the first five options are usually things everyone thinks of, but the second five options are where your creative powers lie. Push yourself to list all ten options.

Here's what I suggest to my students who are stuck in the middle:

1. List ten actions your protagonist can take that are one hundred percent within their control. Be specific and realistic. Saving the entire world is unlikely. Saving a boat full of people is doable.
2. List ten actions your protagonist can take that are dependent on someone else or something else (so

the protagonist only has partial control). This allows for an interplay of cause and effect that will propel the story forward.
3. List ten options that are one hundred percent outside of your protagonist's control, such as the weather. These options may look like coincidences in fiction whereas they may be what actually happens in real life. Therefore, be careful to only add a couple of these to your novel to provide some verisimilitude. Use these options to add conflict and not solve a conflict.
4. List ten options that can NOT happen. Either they have already been tried and have failed or they exist outside the realm of possibilities. For example, if you're writing a historical thriller, you cannot have the protagonist solve the crime through DNA testing since the technology did not exist. You need to adhere to the rules of your story world whatever those rules may be.
5. Once you have your lists, choose one from the three lists of options (one hundred percent protagonist control, fifty percent protagonist control, or zero percent protagonist control) and play the tape forward. Write down a narrative (just telling, no showing) of what would happen if this option was allowed to play out in your novel. It can be simple sentences, such as "If an avalanche happens when the protagonist is on the mountain, then the protagonist will be trapped. If the protagonist is trapped, then someone will have to rescue the protagonist, or they will die. If they are rescued, then they will feel they owe a debt to their rescuer. If they die, then the antagonist (nature) wins."

6. If you like what plays out, then use it in your next scene. If you don't like what plays out, choose another option and go through the "What if/then?" tape again.
7. If you get stuck in the "What if/then?" game, consider your protagonist's response habits (either fight, flight, or freeze) and their strengths, weaknesses, and beliefs. Choose an option that will make your protagonist turn their weakness into a strength or remove their misbelief and reveal their truth.
8. When all else fails, write the ending, and work backward to the middle.

Okay, that's it for today.

Get brainstorming,

Angela

P.S. If you want to play with circumstances, consider writing about a moment of grace in which your protagonist is gifted with something she did not earn, such as hope or forgiveness or something concrete such as money or plane tickets. Let this unexpected good fortune propel the narrative forward through your protagonist's reaction of gratitude or relief.

If you are stuck brainstorming, think smaller, not bigger. Think back on your own life struggles. What moments come to mind? You might want to imagine your protagonist in the future, thinking back on her life. Write down what is revealed to you.

Finally, you can focus on the protagonist's feelings at this juncture. Show the protagonist's frustration or exhaustion. Be specific. Focus on the sensory details. Sometimes by getting inside of your protagonist, you can find the answers.

Word Play

Dear Writer,

You're still having problems.
No worries.
Let's go back to basics.
In my creative writing courses, I teach students the fundamentals of words. I call my technique "playing in the sandbox." When we play in the sandbox, we bring three things with us: our observations of the world around us, our limitless imagination, and our command of the written language.

During the first class, I give my students a sentence and ask them to write a 500-word story using that exact sentence as the opening line. Guess what? Every single time, each story is different. Why does this happen time and again? Because every individual expresses themselves from the viewpoint of their unique combination of genetics (nature), environment (nurture), values (beliefs), knowledge (formal and informal education), observations (sensory input), and memory (recall).

How does any of this information help you in writing the first draft of your novel?

It reassures you that no one can write the exact story you write, not even artificial intelligence.

Are you not convinced?

Here's an exercise I give my students who are stuck writing the rising action of their novels. I've borrowed it from Ray Bradbury's essay "Zen and the Art of Writing."

In the essay, Bradbury preaches:

Work + Relaxation + Don't Think! = First Draft

I preach:

Play + Relaxation + Flow = First Draft

Let me explain the differences.

Bradbury considers writing to be work. He sets a schedule and sticks with it. While I recommend my students treat their writing time as a second job, I usually encounter some resistance from students who are not employed, especially those who are retired. But everyone embraces play. Playing with words is fun, low pressure, and always results in something concrete.

Bradbury used word associations to write the first drafts of his stories. He lists five lines of nouns and sifts through them to find commonalities to build a story. My technique is similar but simplified. I give students pairs of unrelated words and ask them to incorporate the first word in the opening sentence and the last word in the final sentence. Using this technique, I ask them to build the next scene in their novel. You can customize this exercise by limiting your choices to words from your story's universe.

Here's a sample list of words I've given my students:

> deadly/love
> pool/dream
> brother or stepbrother/darkness

mother or mother-in-law/light
city/survival
snow/vacation

Both Bradbury and I agree that once you start working or playing with words, you begin to relax. Your gaze and your shoulders soften. Your breathing slows and your hands pick up the pace, either typing or writing. Eventually, relaxation leads to flow (or "not thinking," as Bradbury suggests). When you are writing and you are relaxed, you are no longer consciously aware of the craft skills you've learned. You are caught up in the joy of creation.

Flow and "not thinking" are synonymous for this lucid state of productivity where you and the story become one. As author Jennifer Lynn Alvarez says, "The story writes me." That internal editor we all carry around inside of us is temporarily silenced.

Try the word association exercise. Set a timer for fifteen minutes. See how long it takes for your muscles to melt and your mind to unwind. Pay attention to the process. See if you can edge into that state of creativity where the words stream from your fingertips as effortlessly as the breath moves through your lungs.

Keep writing,

Angela

P.S. Remember to have fun!

Character Arc

Dear Writer,

    Let's talk about emotion, particularly the emotional journey your protagonist takes in your novel. This journey is typically called "the character arc."
    Before we address the bigger emotional journey, let's start with the smaller one—the emotion of a scene. By showing your character as they are and letting them *feel* on the page through actions, thoughts, and dialogue, you will let readers glimpse the internal world of your protagonist.
    Maybe your protagonist is a lonely widow. Maybe she is shy, too. So instead of going out to meet people, she befriends them online. She develops a deep relationship with these virtual friends in a second life even though in her real life she does not talk to anyone, not even the postal carrier or the people sitting in the same pew at church. But if she wants to end her loneliness after shutting down her computer at night, she must take steps to overcome her shyness and interact with the real people in her life.
    This emotional journey will most likely mirror the narrative arc. The protagonist starts out as one person but must become someone else to achieve her goal. For example, returning to the lonely widow, what type of personality trait will she have to develop to conquer her fear of interacting with people she can see and touch rather

than the ones she deals with online? Computers give her a sense of courage through anonymity. She can be bold and fearless when no one sees who she really is. She can create an online persona, a make-believe version of herself. How can she transfer those skills to her real life? The answer lies in the intersection between her character arc and the narrative arc. What can happen in your novel to motivate her to take the initial step and talk to someone—the postal carrier or a familiar stranger in the same pew at church? Has she developed confidence and courage from her successful online encounters? Show the reader through her appearance, action, and dialogue. Does someone talk to her first? Show the reader how she responds. Countless possibilities exist. Try as many as needed to shape her transformation from shy to outgoing.

If you're stuck, consider breaking down the emotional movement of the story alongside the narrative structure.

Inciting incident—Who is the person at the beginning of the story before they commit to their goal? Focus on personality traits.

Rising action—What are the steps needed to become the person who can achieve this goal? Does she have any secondary traits or hidden traits or false beliefs that are keeping her from realizing her potential or knowing her true self?

Climax—How can you show the person embodying the traits needed to succeed or fail at achieving the goal? Failure often teaches us important life lessons, especially about ourselves. What does the character learn about who she is and what she is capable of through the climactic events in the story?

Denouncement—How can you hint at the person's new trajectory as the story ends?

I know it's a lot to think about and it's hard to articulate the feelings you may experience while undergoing challenges, but that's your objective as a storyteller. You need to create a character readers care about and can root for. One of the ways to achieve this goal is to show the emotional journey the character must take to achieve their goals.

In *Last Chance*, the novel opens with Roman being a pushover. He defers to Paula's advice, since she's a savvy real estate agent who knows what she's talking about when she suggests he sell the inn. During the novel, Roman slowly moves away from his dependency on Paula. Once he decides to keep the inn, he must develop the skills needed to get the business out of debt. Because of this goal, he learns how to stand up for himself and his interests. When Paula breaks up with him, Roman is bereft but not destroyed. He knows he can manage without her assistance by rallying on his own strengths of ingenuity, openness, and curiosity. Additionally, he has a supporting cast of characters to assist him. By the end of the novel, Roman is a man confident in both business and love.

Till next time,

Angela

P.S. Practice writing about your protagonist's emotions in one of these situations:

1. The character undergoes a sorrowful event and realizes she has received a gift from this darkness. Show the transformation.
2. The character has an unexpected emotional response to a situation. For example, in Sylvia Plath's poem "Tulips," the narrator experiences pain from witnessing so much beauty. Show the contradictory feeling in a scene.
3. Place your character in unfamiliar territory and watch her response. Focus on the sensory details to express her emotions.
4. Flip the first exercise on its head by focusing on a happy event that evokes a sense of loss in the character. Maybe the happily-ever-after wedding triggers the fear of losing one's individuality or the advent of parenthood gives rise to the death of carefree recklessness.
5. Flash forward to ten years after your novel ends. Have your protagonist write a letter to you about how the events of the past caused her to be who she is today. Use this letter as an emotional roadmap for your story.

Staying on Track

Dear Writer,

    Today I want to check in with you about your progress.
    By now you're either at the climax of your story or building up to it.
    Typically, once you reach the end of the second act, the rest of the novel is easy to finish. Suddenly, everything makes sense. You know how things will wrap up. But until then, you might struggle to get to that turning point.
    But maybe you're not where you want to be. The beginning is taking too long to write. You're losing your motivation.
    The first time you write a novel, you are learning two things—how to write a longer story and how your writing process works.
    A lot of times my students struggle more with discovering how they write than they do with the story. I'm wondering if that applies to you.
    Have you developed a sustainable writing practice? If not, what have you tried? What succeeded and what failed?
    Sometimes what works one week doesn't work the next. Be flexible. Adjust your schedule to fit your life.

Next, are you setting weekly goals? Have you achieved them? For the things outside of your control, please give yourself some grace. Some things in life are unexpected. Your car breaks. Your in-laws stop by unannounced and stay for a week. You get sick. You lose your job. You get promoted. You fall in love. You break up with someone who means the world to you. Someone close to you dies. These events can derail anyone. If you need time off from writing to deal with these things, please take it. Writing will be here when you get back. Your story won't run away.

For the things you can control, from pushing through resistance to silencing the internal editor, remember to be firm but kind. Everyone struggles at some point during the first draft. The key is to keep writing.

Are you celebrating your successes? Each milestone should be rewarded with a small treat. Did you make your weekly word count or scene goal? Go buy yourself an ice cream cone or play an extra game of tennis—whatever feels appropriate.

When you miss the mark, evaluate where you went off course and how you can get back on track.

Do you need an accountability partner? Do you need a brainstorming session?

Do you need a break?

A former student spent one month writing 2,000 words each day. By the end of the month, she wondered why she couldn't keep up the pace. When I asked her what had changed, she mentioned she started a new job and had a baby. New job? That's tough. And a new baby? Almost impossible. When did she sleep? After discussing what goals were realistic given the changes in her life, she agreed to relax her goals and prioritize self-care. If you're burned out, you can't write.

Take care of yourself, those you love, and your other responsibilities.

Writing is supposed to be a joyful *part* of your life. It is not meant to be your *whole* life.

Don't suffer for your art.

Eat well. Exercise. Get plenty of sleep. Spend time with family and friends. Keep your house clean and organized.

Be realistic with your writing goals. High expectations always lead to disappointment. Disappointment kills your spirit. A deadened spirit flattens motivation. Without motivation, you are more likely to abandon your manuscript.

Do. Not. Give. Up.

Keep writing.

A balanced life of moderation serves your writing well. If you cherish your family but lock yourself in the spare bedroom while neglecting everyone around you, your words may flow but your life around you will dry up.

My worst memory as a mother was when my adult daughter saw a notebook that read, "F* off, I'm writing," and said, "When I was growing up, I hated Daddy saying, 'Don't bother Mommy. She's writing.' I always wanted to break down the office door. I wanted you to play with me."

So, avoid regrets. Keep an open-door policy for your children.

But treat your writing with respect. Set healthy boundaries. If you're self-employed, book your writing time like any other appointment. Don't let clients bully you into surrendering that hour or so a day for their benefit. When I was working as a full-time real estate agent, I used to arrange my schedule to suit my clients' needs for fear of losing business. Once I prioritized my life, including my family, friends, and hobbies, I not only increased my business but attracted better-paying clients who respected my time. Train your clients. Your wallet will thank you.

That's why I asked you earlier to create a schedule. Carve out dedicated time for your first draft like you would for a doctor's appointment or a child's recital. If you treat your writing with respect, it will flourish. Author Jennifer Lynn Alvarez went from housewife to published novelist by treating her writing like a job. She turned down volunteer work she normally said yes to so she could write while her three children were in school.

But what if you get stuck staring at the blank page during your writing time?

Pick an exercise from this book, set a timer for five minutes, and write.

Do not think about the quality of the writing.

Just get words down.

You can fix everything later.

Occasionally the universe will gift you with a polished gem of a story like it did with my flash fiction "Stolen Grief." Most of the time writing is work just like Bradbury said. Do the work, and your writing will get better.

Remember every writer has doubts.

Every writer has failures.

That is normal. It's part of being human.

Imposter syndrome doesn't disappear with success. Go online and look up your favorite authors. Every single one of them writes about their struggles, either in a tweet or blog or an interview.

Finally, don't wait for validation. The publishing world might never shine its gaze on your story. Or readers might post negative reviews. Sales may climb or plummet. None of that matters, except to your ego. But if you write from your ego, you're writing to please an audience. And no one can please everyone all the time. Write to please yourself. If you're not happy with the story, why would you expect a reader to be?

Keep writing,

Angela

P.S. Try this: when a stranger asks what you do, tell them you're a writer. How does it feel?

The more you tell others you're a writer, the more real it will feel for you. It took me years before I felt comfortable calling myself a writer. I wanted some proof to show others such as a published short story. Don't wait for proof. If you write, you are a writer. The proof will come if you put in the time and effort.

Writing the End

Dear Writer,

If you remember from one of my earlier letters, the classic Aristotelian plot consists of twenty-five percent the beginning, fifty percent the middle, and twenty-five percent the ending.

Today we'll discuss writing the ending.

What happens during the end?

The climax. This is the moment the reader has been anticipating since they read the opening line. The protagonist faces her biggest challenge. The result of that challenge answers the story's major dramatic question.

Before this moment, the rest of the story will start wrapping up. Typically, subplots or parallel plots will be resolved.

Why?

Because after the climax, the reader loses interest.

If you can tease out the tension as long as possible while tidying up the minor conflicts with secondary characters, you'll be on your way to writing a satisfying conclusion.

What makes for a satisfying ending? The protagonist solves her problem.

Resist the urge to save the day with a knight in shining armor. Readers expect the protagonist has grown enough to fix her own life rather than rely on someone or something outside of herself.

It's okay if the protagonist fails as long as you have planted the seeds for her failure along the way.

The same is true for success.

According to Aristotle, a good ending feels "surprising but inevitable." If you are not surprised, your reader will not be surprised.

How do you surprise yourself?

You write out three or more possible conclusions to the big moment. Then you consider everything that has happened beforehand and everything that happens thereafter and choose the climax that seems most likely.

It may change once you write it.

When I was writing *Last Chance*, I knew Roman would save the inn, but I didn't know how until I wrote my way into the final scenes.

After the climax, the denouncement follows. Typically, it's only a chapter or two to give closure to the story by answering any lingering questions a reader might have.

Sometimes an epilogue satisfies this requirement. You skip forward in time and show the reader the protagonist in the future. I used this technique in *Last Chance* to show Roman marrying Lian one year after he rescued the inn.

How will you feel once you write those final words, "The End"?

Sometimes you feel relief.

Sometimes you feel empty and used by the muse.

Sometimes you feel joy.

Sometimes you feel grief.

You may feel all these emotions and more during the days or weeks following the completion of a first draft.

It makes sense if you think about it. You've spent weeks or months or maybe even years with these characters in this world. They may have become your closest friends.

In *Writing Down the Bones*, Natalie Goldberg chronicles the moments after finishing her book. She says, "We have an idea that success is a happy occasion. Success can also be lonely, isolating, disappointing. It makes sense that it is everything."

Let yourself feel whatever you feel once your first draft is finished.

Then go out and celebrate your success!

I'm proud of you,

Angela

P.S. I typically buy a sheet cake with "First Draft Finished" written in frosting to share with my family to thank them for their support and patience.

What's Next?

Dear Writer,

While I never intended to cover the scope of revision and publishing within these letters, I do want to address these topics briefly. Why? Because I am often asked about the steps you should take after finishing a first draft.

First, you need to celebrate. You are one of the three percent who finish writing a novel. Do something BIGGER than you did to celebrate meeting each of your milestones. Like I previously stated in the last letter to you, I celebrate by buying a cake to share with my family to thank them for their love and support during the drafting process.

Next, you need to take a four-to-six-week break before you revisit your manuscript. Sometimes a longer break is needed. Trust your judgment.

What do you do during this period? You have several options. If you feel so inspired, you may start writing your next novel. Or you may write smaller pieces like poetry or flash fiction. If you don't feel creative, spend time replenishing your reserves through engaging in art passively through visiting museums or attending readings. Finally, you may choose to do nothing. I have stepped away from my writing practice as needed to refill my cup, so I may return. I call this process lying fallow, which is a term I borrowed from the late poet David Bromige who I met at a poetry reading.

But if you feel a need to fill the time with something related to your novel, you may decide to either research those details missing from your first draft or investigate the publishing process.

I had a student who asked on the first night of class, "Why don't we talk about publishing? If we're going to make money at this gig, shouldn't that be front and center?"

That same student told me on the last night of class that she had been hoping to write a cozy mystery with a sweet romantic subplot, but her protagonist took over and she ended up writing a gritty hard-core detective novel instead. If that student had pitched her yet-to-be-written cozy romantic mystery novel and received a contract, she would have failed to deliver a publishable manuscript. Why? Because the publisher bought a cozy romantic mystery, and not a gritty hard-core detective novel. This example is the primary reason I suggest forgetting about the publishing market during your first draft. You don't know the end product.

But now that your first draft is complete, it's okay to discuss your publishing options.

If you want to sell to a big commercial publisher, your best bet is to find a literary agent to represent you and your novel. You can find a literary agent in several ways. Check the acknowledgment page of authors who write in the same genre to see if they thank their agents. Search for agents by specialty through the Association of American Literary Agents. Attend writers' conferences. Ask your fellow authors for referrals.

If you want to sell to a small press, you can represent yourself. Query the publisher directly. Always check the publisher's website for submission guidelines.

You can also hire a hybrid publisher who will publish your novel for a fee. This service is different than subsidy publishing because hybrid publishers typically come from traditional presses and only accept manuscripts that meet current publishing standards. If in doubt, check with the Better Business Bureau or contact some of the authors who have worked with the publisher you are considering. Also, buy one of their books to see if the quality matches your expectations.

Finally, you can self-publish. Taking this route, you would hire all the team members needed to produce your book, from editor to cover artist to marketing director. Or you can do these tasks on your own. The choice is yours. Reedsy is a good online resource to find professionals to help you with this do-it-yourself process.

No matter what you choose—writing a new novel, attending literary events, researching missing information for your novel or studying the publishing landscape—enjoy the time away.

Fondly,

Angela

P.S. You may want to explore other art forms during your fallow period. I often paint between writing projects.

Final Thoughts

Dear Writer,

Thank you for spending time with me through these letters. I've enjoyed communicating with you.

Before I go, I'd like to leave you with some final thoughts.

Please, don't send your initial draft to anyone for feedback. It's not ready yet.

When will it be ready?

After you've gone through the manuscript with fresh eyes and discovered how you want to shape the final story.

Here's my process:

I read my first draft as a reader would. I highlight any place that takes me out of the story or diverts me away from the premise. A few side tangents are fine if they are subplots or character development. A lot of discursive storytelling is not. Afterward, I write a synopsis, which I use as a roadmap for revision. Then I outline the beats of the story. I cut out any scenes that no longer work and paste them into a document I save as "Notes" on my computer. Finally, I go through the manuscript and write anything needed to connect those beats together into a coherent story with a beginning, middle, and end. After letting that second draft cool for a couple of weeks, I reread the manuscript. I double-check that my revision flows, both for the narrative arc and the character arc. If it's intact, then I go through and correct any grammatical and spelling errors. The third manuscript is the one I send to readers. Right now, I have a friend with whom I meet once a month for feedback. We read, critique, and discuss improvements needed. You may have such a friend or a trusted reader in your circle of influence. You can also hire a professional editor who has experience editing in your genre.

Your revision process may look different from mine. That's okay. As always, you need to do what works best for you and your story.

Before I go, I want to check in with you about the lessons you've learned throughout this process.

Have you developed a sustainable writing practice?

Have you conquered any psychological barriers that thwart your writing process?

Have you learned to leave your ego and your internal editor at the door while writing the first draft?

Have you gained confidence in your writing skills?

Have you learned to treat yourself kindly when you fail to meet your weekly writing goals?

Have you adjusted your expectations, set healthy boundaries, and discovered the values that drive you as a writer?

Have you learned how to balance a creative project with your life?

Have you discovered joy throughout this journey?

Whatever you've learned, please share your thoughts with me at www.angelalamwriter.com. I love hearing from my students.

Writing the first draft of a novel is a solitary process. I hope these letters have nudged you onward on days you didn't feel like writing (and we all have those days, even me) or guided you when you felt lost (and we all get lost on our way every now and then no matter how many books we write). Most importantly, I hope you have developed new techniques and boosted your writing confidence.

Best wishes,

Angela

P.S. Don't say this book you've just written is your one and only book. Why? You're a writer. Writers write. Who knows where your next story will take you?

List of Resources

Books:

Refuse to be Done by Matt Bell (First Draft and Revision)

Zen and the Art of Writing by Ray Bradbury (The Writing Life and Word Association)

Save the Cat! Writes a Novel by Jessica Brody (Plot, Outlining, Beat Sheets)

Mastering Deep Point of View by Alice Gaines (Point of View and Voice)

Writing Down the Bones by Natalie Goldberg (Developing a Writing Practice)

Expectation Hangover by Christine Hassler (Overcoming Perfectionism and Other Psychological Barriers)

On Writing by Stephen King (The Writing Life)

Bird by Bird by Anne Lamott (Developing a Writing Practice)

The War of Art by Steven Pressfield (Resistance/Procrastination/Motivation/Inspiration)

Letters to a Young Poet by Rainer Maria Rilke (The Writing Life)

Make a Scene Revised and Expanded by Jordan Rosenfeld (Showing Versus Telling)

Techniques of the Selling Writer by Dwight V. Swain (Scene and Summary/Selling)

Courses and Community:

NaNoWriMo— National Novel Writing Month

Novel II First Draft—Part 1 at Gotham Writers Workshop

After the First Draft:

BookLife (Indie website affiliated with Publishers Weekly)

Jane Friedman (Craft and Publishing Advice)

Publishers Weekly (Business of Writing)

Reedsy (Hub for finding editors, designers, and marketers for your manuscript)

Letters to a First-Time Novelist 96

Acknowledgments

Thank you to Gotham Writers Workshop for the opportunity to coach writing students from start to finish. I am forever grateful for being of service to hundreds of students.

Thank you to my family, friends, and readers for your love and support throughout the years.

About the Author

Angela Lam is the author of several novels, a novella, two memoirs, and two short story collections. She is available for one-on-one coaching, developmental editing, or ten-week courses through Gotham Writers Workshop.

www.ingramcontent.com/pod-product-compliance
Lightning Source LLC
LaVergne TN
LVHW091311080426
835510LV00007B/473